Geography Starts

SEAS AND OCEANS

Andy Owen
and
Miranda Ashwell

Heinemann Interactive Library
Des Plaines, Illinois

© 1998 Reed Educational & Professional Publishing
Published by Heinemann Interactive Library,
an imprint of Reed Educational & Professional Publishing,
1350 East Touhy Avenue, Suite 240 West
Des Plaines, IL 60018

Designed by Susan Clarke
Illustrations by Oxford Illustrators (maps pp.23, 25, 27)
Printed in Hong Kong

02 01 00 99 98
10 9 8 7 6 5 4 3 2 1

Library of Congress Cataloging-in-Publication Data
Owen, Andy, 1961-
     Seas and oceans / Andy Owen and Miranda Ashwell.
        p.   cm. — (Geography starts)
     Includes bibliographical references and index.
     Summary: An introduction to the seas and oceans of the world and
the impact of people on them.
        ISBN 1-57572-608-4 (lib. bdg.)
        1. Ocean—Juvenile literature.   [1. Ocean.]   I. Ashwell,
Miranda, 1957- . II. Title.   III. Series: Owen, Andy, 1961-
Geography starts.
GC21.5.094   1998
551.46—dc21
                                                97-34422
                                                CIP
                                                AC

Acknowledgments
The Publishers would like to thank the following for permission to reproduce photographs:
Aerofilms, p.17; Australian Picture Library/J. Carnemolla, p.4; Geoslides, p.8; Images Colour
Library, p.6; Kos Picture Source, p.7; NRSC pp.22, 24, 26; Oxford Scientific Films/Ian West,
p.19; Planet Earth, p.14 (Jiri Lochman); Rex Features/Huw Evans, p.18; Robert Harding
Picture Library/Ian Griffiths, p.13; Royal Geographical Society, p.15; Telegraph/F.P.G., p.9, p.10
(Norbert Wu), p.11 (Kurt Amsler); Tony Stone, pp.5, 12, p.20 (George Grogoriou), p.21
(Stephan Munday)

Cover photograph: Tony Stone/Warren Bolster

Our thanks to Betty Root for her comments in the preparation of this book.

Every effort has been made to contact copyright holders of any material reproduced in this
book. Any omissions will be rectified in subsequent printings if notice is given to the publisher.

Some words are shown in bold, **like this**. You can find
out what they mean by looking in the glossary.

Contents

Seas and Oceans

Oceans are very large bodies of salt water. The water is very deep and the waves can be very big.

This boat will take many weeks to reach land.

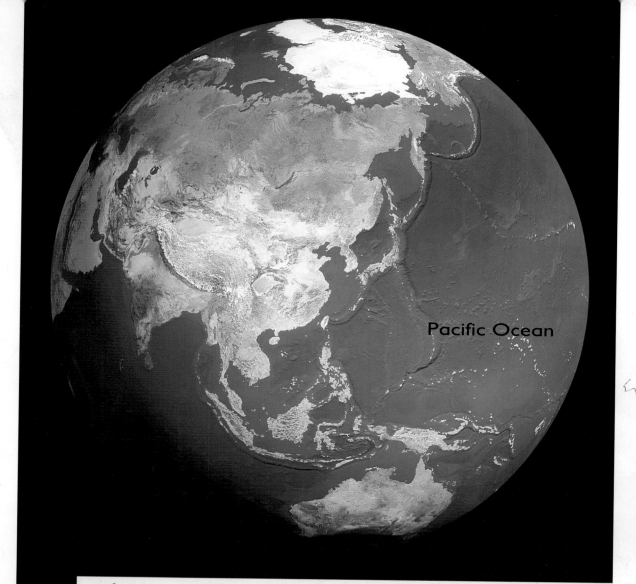

Pacific Ocean

photo of the world from space

Most of the world is covered by seas and oceans. The blue in this photo is the Pacific Ocean. It is the largest ocean in the world.

Islands

Land with water all around it is called an island. There are many islands in the world's oceans.

This island is in the Pacific Ocean.

This island is in the Atlantic Ocean.

Islands can be large or small. People live in towns and cities on some islands. Many islands have no people at all.

Cold and Warm Seas

Most of this iceberg is hidden under water.

Water in the Arctic Ocean is so cold it turns to ice. These large blocks of ice are called icebergs. They float in the water.

The Great Barrier Reef grows in the sea off Australia. The coral is growing in the light blue water.

A coral reef is a large mound made from the skeletons of millions of tiny animals. Coral reefs often grow in warm and shallow parts of oceans.

9

Deep and Shallow

Most seas and oceans are very deep. The water gets darker and colder as the sea gets deeper.

Scientists go to the bottom of deep seas in a diving bell.

Divers hold their breaths
to swim in shallow water.

The sea is often shallow close to land.
Fish, coral, and seaweed living near
the surface get a lot of light.

Waves

Strong winds and huge waves make a storm at sea.

Strong winds whip the water into waves. Waves get larger as the wind blows harder. Boats and ships get tossed about by the storm.

Large waves can be dangerous.

The wind pushes waves toward the coast. The waves tumble and crash onto land. A crashing wave is called a **breaker.**

13

Cliffs

Waves splash against the cliffs and wear away the rock. The shapes of the cliffs were made by pounding waves.

These high cliffs are very steep.

Buildings fell down when part of this cliff fell away.

Over many years, waves weaken the rocks at the bottom of the cliff. Then the top of the cliff falls onto the beach below.

Beaches

Waves roll sand and stones around in the sea. After many years, the stones become smooth and round.

This beach is full of smooth stones and pebbles.

Waves carry sand along beaches. When the waves slow down, the sand falls. A **sand bar** is made.

This sand bar is in England.

Pollution

Oil leaking from ships floats on water. This is called an **oil slick**. The oil is carried by the waves.

It takes many people and boats to clean up an oil slick.

These people are cleaning oil off a beach.

Waves carry the oil slick onto the beach.
It harms **wildlife** on the coast.

Safe Places

Harbor walls are built to keep out wind and waves. During a storm, small boats are safe inside a **harbor**.

harbor wall

Only small boats can use this harbor.

Large ships can only use harbors with very deep water. Places where ships load and unload are called ports.

Sydney harbor in Australia

Ocean Map 1

This photo was taken from an airplane. You can see a small **harbor**. There are some boats inside the harbor.

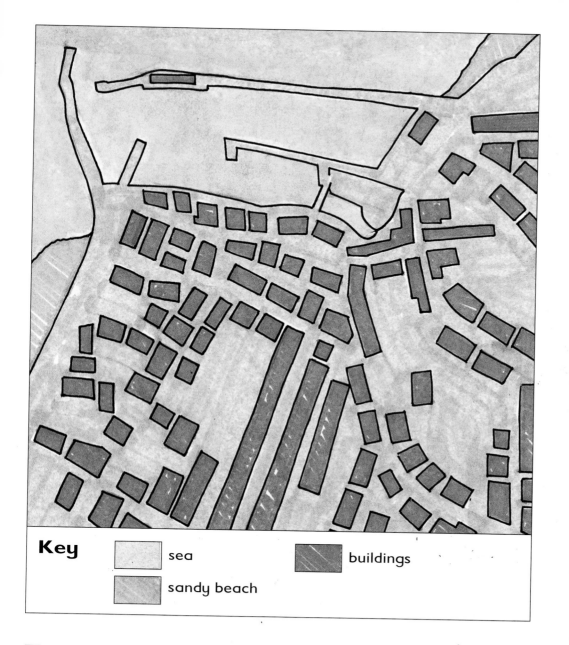

Key

sea

buildings

sandy beach

This is a map of the same harbor. The **harbor wall** is shown. A map never shows boats because they move from place to place.

Ocean Map 2

This photo shows the same place. The **harbor** looks smaller, and you can see beaches on both sides of the harbor.

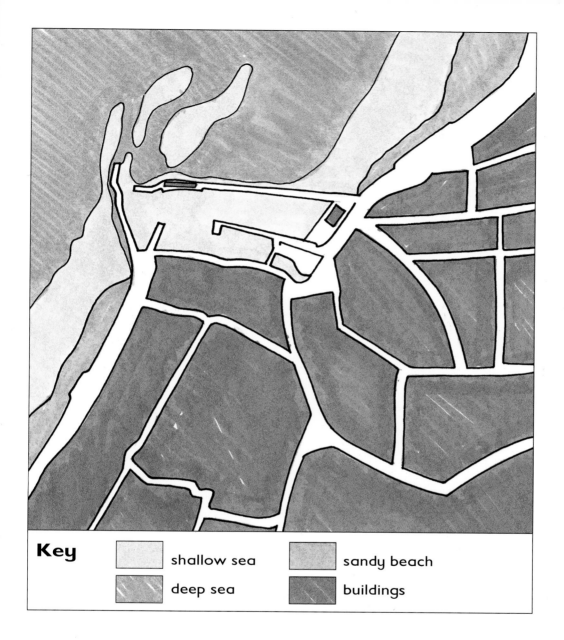

Key

	shallow sea		sandy beach
	deep sea		buildings

A key helps you to understand the map. It describes the things that are on the photo. Light blue shows the shallow water of the harbor. Dark blue shows the deeper water.

Ocean Map 3

You can see even more of the sea and town in this photo. The sun is shining on the water, which makes the waves easy to see.

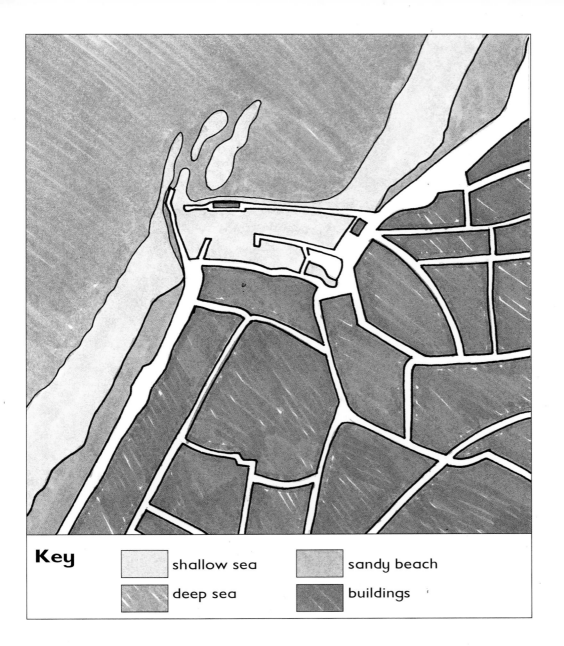

Key

shallow sea	sandy beach
deep sea	buildings

The waves are not shown on the map.
This is because waves are always moving
and changing.

Amazing Ocean Facts

The Great Barrier Reef in Australia is the longest **coral reef** in the world. The reef has been growing for 12 million years.

The Great Barrier Reef is 1,250 miles (2,010 kilometers long.)

The largest ocean in the world is the Pacific Ocean. The deepest part of the ocean is the Mariana **Trench.**

This valley is more than 7 miles (11 kilometers) deep.

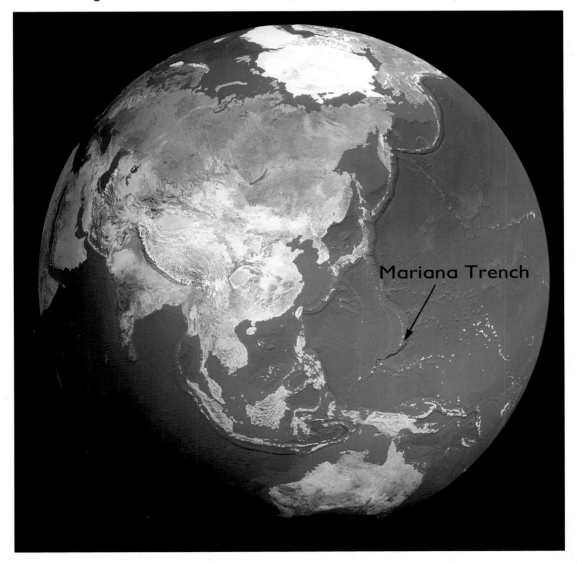

Mariana Trench

Glossary

breaker wave that crashes onto the land

harbor place on the coast where boats and ships are safe from rough seas

harbor walls strong walls that stop waves and rough seas from coming into the harbor

oil slick large patch of oil floating on the water

sand bar strip of sand in shallow water

trench long, narrow opening in the earth

wildlife plants, animals, fish, and birds

More Books to Read

Carter, Katherine. *Oceans.*
Danbury, Conn: Childrens Press, 1982.

DeBeauregard, Diane C. *The Blue Planet: Seas and Oceans.* Ossining, NY: Young Discovery Library, 1989.

DeMuth, Patricia. *Way Down Deep.*
New York: Putnam, 1995.

Malfatti, Patricia. *Look Inside the Ocean.*
New York: Putnam, 1993.

Souza, D. M. *Powerful Waves.*
Minneapolis: The Lerner Group, 1992.

The Sea. Austin, Tex: Raintree Steck-Vaughn, 1986.

Sea Life. New York: Dorling Kindersley, 1994.

Index